# Green Diesel Days

# Derek Huntriss

# Green Diesel Days

Ian Allan
PUBLISHING

## Dedication:

To my mother Mabel, for supporting my enthusiasm in my formative years, for sitting on endless platform ends watching trains, and for being there for me throughout my life — ALWAYS!!!

## Acknowledgments:

I would like to take this opportunity to acknowledge the work of the officers and members of the RCTS (Railway Correspondence & Travel Society) who have been faithfully recording the railway scene in Great Britain and overseas for many years and who have collectively amassed a vast store of knowledge. This knowledge has enabled the society to published a series of widely acclaimed detailed locomotive histories which are regarded as the definitive reference books for researchers and modellers alike. Their monthly journal *The Railway Observer*, which has been in continuous publication since 1928, contains a wealth of railway minutiae from correspondents throughout the UK which may otherwise have been lost. A number of the captions written in this book are based on information recorded in these journals.

Most railway photographers reserved their film for recording the operations of surviving steam locomotives, colour pictures of early diesels being few and far between. I offer my sincere thanks to all those who have willingly contributed their irreplaceable material for inclusion in this title. We all owe them a debt of gratitude for recording a period of railway history which is now as remote as the steam age itself.

All pictures in this title credited to the late Derek Cross appear with the kind permission of his son, David. I must also convey deep appreciation for the guidance of John Edgington who gladly shared his in-depth knowledge when he pointed out many details of interest in the pictures seen in this title which otherwise would have escaped my attention. Sincere thanks to John are also offered for his help in proof reading the title.

Derek Huntriss
Coventry
*May 2005*

## Bibliography:

Stephen Batty: *British Rail at Work - West Yorkshire;* Ian Allan
Colin Boocock: *British Railways in Colour 1948-1968;* Ian Allan
Murray Brown: *Rail Portfolios - The Deltics;* Ian Allan
A. K. Butlin: *Diesel Disposal;* Coorlea Publishing
Hugh Dady: *Diesels on the Western Region;* Ian Allan
H. G. Forsythe: *Men of the Diesels;* Atlantic Transport Publishing
Ken Hoole: *Trains in Trouble - Vol. 3;* Atlantic Transport Publishers
L. A. Nixon: *BR Colour Album;* Ian Allan
Robert Stephens: *Diesel Pioneers;* Atlantic Transport Publishing
*British Rail — Main Line Gradient Profiles;* Ian Allan
*British Railways Pre-Grouping Atlas and Gazetteer;* Ian Allan
*Diesel & Electric Loco Register;* Platform 5 Publishing
Other Publications: *Backtrack, Modern Railways, Railway Magazine, Railway World, RCTS Railway Observer, Traction Magazine, Trains Illustrated, The World of Trains.*

*Front cover:*
**Released from Doncaster Works on 6 November 1961, English Electric 'Deltic' No D9016 made its first journey in revenue earning service on the following day at the head of 1A47, the 1.30pm up 'Heart of Midlothian' from Edinburgh to Kings Cross. Still to be named, No D9016 is seen on 24 May 1962, also with 1A47, 2½ miles west of Reston, north of Berwick-on-Tweed.** *Mike Mensing*

*Rear cover, top:*
**With much ex-GWR 'furniture' still in evidence Beyer-Peacock 'Hymek' 1,700hp B-B No D7072 stands at Kemble on 25 May 1963 with a Paddington to Gloucester train.** *Bryan Hicks*

*Rear cover, bottom:*
**The classic view of an early evening departure from St Pancras sees ex-works 'Peak' No D114 waiting to leave with the down 'Robin Hood' service to Nottingham on 31 August 1961. One year earlier the popular 5.30pm ex-St Pancras had become the 5.25pm 'Robin Hood', omitting the Luton stop, whilst the former 4.45pm 'Robin Hood', introduced in 1959, was replaced by an un-named 4.35pm semi-fast to Nottingham.** *Cliff Woodhead*

*Half-title page:*
**Freshly outshopped 'Warship' No D827 *Kelly* stands outside Swindon Works 'A' shop in February 1965. Later that year on 10 October, No D827 broke new ground by working the 8.45am Waterloo to Southampton Western Docks boat train, which was routed via Cobham, Guildford, Havant and Netley.** *Roy Hobbs*

*Title page:*
**Much to the disappointment of the photographer who was expecting steam haulage of the down 'Bournemouth Belle', this 1967 view taken near Beaulieu Road sees Brush-Sulzer Type 4 No D1926 at the head of the train. This formation has a 'BG' (Brake Gangwayed Parcels Van) at each end of the train, earlier Pullman formations using a Brake Parlour Car.** *Derek Penney*

First published 2005

ISBN 0 7110 3066 9

Published by Ian Allan Publishing

An imprint of Ian Allan Publishing Ltd, Hersham, Surrey, KT12 4RG;

and printed by Ian Allan Printing Ltd., Hersham, Surrey, KT12 4RG.

Code: 0508/C2

Visit the Ian Allan Publishing website at www.ianallanpublishing.com

# Contents

A powerful picture of the prototype English Electric 2,700hp Co-Co No DP2 as it powers the 1.35pm Euston to Perth through Harrow & Wealdstone station in 1962. By mid-July 1963 No DP2 was transferred from the LMR to the East Coast route at the manufacturer's request to allow its direct comparison with the English Electric 'Deltics'. *Geoff Rixon*

# Introduction

In 1955, the British Transport Commission published its Railway Modernisation Plan. At last, Britain was to have a train service as good as any in the world, and the Press, the public and the government were all duly impressed. What no one had foreseen were the problems that lay ahead. The following is a quotation from the Modernisation Plan: 'The (British Transport) Commission have decided that major changes in the forms of motive power on British Railways must be effected, involving a widespread changeover from steam to electricity and diesel power. These motive power developments are a prerequisite of the improved quality of service that will be required by industry and the travelling public in future, and which the Commission are determined to provide. Equally, however, the changes will lead to economies in operation ... (and an) all-round increase in railway efficiency.'

It was with these words that the death knell of steam traction was sounded. The merits of the new forms of motive power were eulogised by the authors. Obviously electric traction was seen as the ideal but dieselisation 'could be effected as quickly as the diesel units could be built'. The decision was that both electrification and dieselisation should proceed apace, and a substantial conversion programme costing £345 million (at 1954 prices!) was set out. The Plan was to cover a 15-year period and during this time there was to be an improvement of track and signalling; modernisation of passenger rolling stock and station facilities; and the recasting of goods services, especially through the fitting of continuous brakes on all wagons.

The 1955 Plan provided for the introduction of 2,500 locomotives, with initial orders for 171 machines. In 1956, for the first time, more diesel locomotives were built than steam. Several of the Pilot Scheme orders were for batches of 10 or 20 locomotives, forsaking the construction of a prototype, a mistake which BR later came to regret.

Maintenance of these early engines presented a major problem, many engines having to share outdated and unsuitable facilities with steam. This problem was addressed by the construction of purpose-built diesel maintenance depots, the first of these being in north London at Devons Road. Most coaching stock was then not equipped for electrical train heating, so many diesel locomotives were fitted with train-heating boilers, which often took their weight over the specified axle loading and restricted their route availability. Other weight problems with the early designs became apparent when working loose coupled freight, runaways occurring because of inadequate braking power. This problem was remedied by the building of specially constructed brake tenders which remained in use pending the disappearance of loose coupled freight working.

Prior to the introduction of a standard traction plan for the whole of BR, the Western Region pursued its own policy of introducing diesel hydraulic locomotives, copying the best of available German technology. However, once standardisation policies were conceived in the mid-1960s, the hydraulics were among the first casualties of the diesel era.

It can be asked — was the Modernisation Plan a success? Had the plan not existed the railway would have been in a far worse state. It can be ascertained that half of the expenditure under the Plan was to undertake essential work deferred since the war years. With the huge increase in private motoring mistakes were certainly made in the traffic estimates, the motorway building programme and the container revolution were not foreseen. Some would say that the Plan should have come after the reshaping carried out in the 1960s by the new chairman, Dr Richard Beeching, since money was spent on parts of the system that the Doctor decided to axe.

With hindsight, BR would have benefited from the evolution of standard types from its pilot scheme designs. As it was, its policies resulted in a wide variety of non-standard types of varying quality, and much time, effort and money was wasted. However, to the enthusiast, the transition from steam was fascinating, with a number of diesel classes appearing and disappearing within a short time span. Experiments with liveries, too, provided colourful contrasts with the grime and matt black of the ageing steam fleet, and in this title I have, where possible, portrayed the earliest liveries of each type.

*Top:*
SR/English Electric Co 1,750/2,000hp 1Co-Co1 prototype No 10201, is seen inside the roundhouse at Willesden (1A) MPD on 25 March 1961. Its original black livery had been replaced with lined out BR green in July 1956, the aluminium numbers being painted cream. *T. B. Owen*

*Above:*
Clayton Equipment Co 900hp Bo-Bo Type 1 No D8531 is seen outside Polmadie (66A) MPD on 3 June 1963. Built for use on the Scottish Region, No D8500 had arrived at Polmadie on 10 September 1962, replacing the veteran 'Jumbos' on their various trip workings. *Ray Reed*

*Top:*
**This 24 August 1956 picture sees 'Derby Lightweight' single car unit M79901 waiting to depart from Buckingham. Two experimental single-car units were built for branch line service on the LMR as part of a comprehensive 1954 order for more conventional DMUs.** *John Edgington*

*Above:*
**English Electric Type 4 No D207 climbs Gamston Bank, near Retford, with an up working in 1958. The allocation of the first batch of 10 locomotives was shared between Stratford for Great Eastern line duties and Hornsey for use on the Great Northern main line.** *Derek Penney*

English Electric Type 4 No D374 climbs towards Shap Wells with what is probably a Birmingham to Glasgow train in October 1964. Introduced quickly by the LMR on to principal express workings the class was eventually supplanted by the English Electric Co 'D400s'. *T. B. Owen*

A classic view depicting the transition from steam to diesel as trains pass near Stoneycombe, Devon, on 3 September 1960. A North British Locomotive Co 'D63xx' B-B pilots an unidentified 'Hall' class 4-6-0 with the 6.40am St Austell to Birmingham as it passes No D6318 piloting 'Warship' No D807 *Caradoc* on the overnight Manchester to Penzance. Contemporary reports suggested that there were insufficient trains capable of being worked by a single engine, but in practice the use of two locomotives in tandem was preferred in case of failure in one engine. *Peter W. Gray*

Forerunners of the HST, the five 'Blue Pullman' train sets, introduced in 1959, were designed jointly by BR and Metropolitan Cammell, and were intended to emulate both continental and airline practice. Here a WR eight-car set forms the 'Bristol Pullman' passing Tilehurst in 1961. *Derek Penney*

# ONE

# Western Region

When considering the type of diesel locomotive that would best suit their needs, the engineers on the Western Region (WR) viewed with horror the heavyweight diesel-electrics already running and with an eye on the steep gradients west of Newton Abbot they decided that their requirements would be best met by a British-built version of the much lighter 'V200' class diesel-hydraulics already running in West Germany. Hydraulic enthusiasts argued that the diesel-electric principle of converting mechanical power at the engine crankshaft into electrical power, and back again in the traction motors, was a circuituous method of achieving a simple object. It was this reasoning rather than re-estabilishing the former GWR independence that provided the testing ground for the diesel-hydraulic locomotives. Paddington would have been delighted to buy the 'V200' locomotives virtually off the shelf but they were very much out of gauge for running on BR. To this end the Western Region entered into a licensing agreement with Krauss-Maffei and set about adapting all of the 'V200' locomotives into the BR loading gauge.

The outcome of this arrangement was the production of two classes of Bo-Bo locomotives, the Swindon-built Class 42 ('Warships') which used Maybach engines and an alternative Mekydro transmission which first appeared in 1958, and the Class 43 which utilised MAN engines with the Voith transmission. These locomotives were constructed by the North British Locomotive Company which built the MAN engines under licence.

BR was quick to realise that locomotives of the 2,000-2,200hp power range were not sufficiently powerful to meet the aspirations of the timetable planners. The WR then set out to design a more powerful diesel-hydraulic locomotive, learning from the lessons of operating the existing classes.

It was felt that the MAN engine had been most troublesome whereas the Maybach engine was giving good results. The Voith transmission was clearly superior to its Mekydro alternative, giving an almost stepless output.

The new locomotive, which later became the Class 52 'Western', utilised two Maybach MD655 engines each developing 1,350hp, each using Voith transmissions, having three torque convertors. At this time the WR had built the best components into one machine which would be capable of working any anticipated passenger duties.

As early as 1962, the Western Region had been instructed to bring its policies into line with other regions and in 1967 a high-level decision had been made to rationalise the number and different types of BR diesels, which led to the planned withdrawal of all diesel-hydraulics by 1974. The 'D600s' had succumbed by the end of 1967 and 29 of the North British Locomotive Co 1,000/1,100hp B-Bs were withdrawn before the end of 1969. There was a reprieve for this class in 1970 when no further examples were withdrawn, but they resumed in 1971, the last two of the type being officially withdrawn on 1 January 1972. At the beginning of 1973 only the 'Westerns' remained intact but by the spring of that year the first casualty went to the dump. It was to be two and a half years later than planned, on 26 February 1977, that the last four 'Westerns' completed their working lives on BR, ending another stage in the unique history of the Western Region.

The Great Western Railway had also been the first of Britain's 'Big Four' railway companies to make any significant use of the diesel railcar on some cross-country and rural routes. Such was the success of the buffet-equipped 'Flying Bananas' in the 1930s that they had soon to be replaced by locomotive-hauled trains. These early GWR cars were not equipped for multiple-unit working but further GWR railcars introduced in the 1940s were capable of hauling a tail-load and operating in multiple. Four of these cars were fitted with gangwayed ends and ran as two-car units thus heralding the day of the cross-country DMU.

More than 15 years passed before the BR Modernisation Plan of 1955 brought new DMU designs to the Western Region with vehicles by Pressed Steel, Gloucester RC&W, and the BR works at Swindon and Derby. Some of these sets were high-density non-gangwayed units for suburban use, but the plan also called for gangwayed, lavatory-equipped sets for cross-country running between major centres on the Western Region.

*Above:*

**North British built 'Warship' No D834** *Pathfinder* **arrives at Penzance in May 1965. The Post Office red livery of the GPO carriage contrasts markedly with the darker BR standard maroon livery of the main train. The highest numbered milepost in Britain is on the retaining wall — this sign read 326½ miles from Paddington via Bristol.** *Cliff Woodhead*

*Below:*

**North British Locomotive Co 2,000hp A1A-A1A No D603** *Conquest* **passes a centre-pivoted calling on arm as it enters Truro station with the up 'Cornish Riviera Express' on 15 May 1959. With the introduction of the 'D800' class, the A1A-A1As were displaced from their principal duties on the West of England main line.** *M. Mensing*

*Above:*
**Humble duties for 'Warship' No D816 *Eclipse* as it enters Lostwithiel with a china clay train on 20 July 1960. After the first batch of this class entered traffic, WR drivers experienced rough riding at speeds over 75mph. Tests in 1959/60 attributed this problem to the bogie design and subsequent modifications successfully overcame it.** *R. C. Riley*

*Below:*
**Utilising the 'Cornishman' stock, this picture taken on Sunday 6 August 1961 depicts No D816 *Eclipse* as it climbs Dainton Bank with the 10.10am Wolverhampton to Penzance. Apart from the bogie problems, the 'D800s' gave the WR excellent service with top speeds often in excess of the authorised 90mph.** *Hugh Ballantyne*

Berry Head can be seen in the background of this picture showing DMU set LA301 as it works the 6.35pm from Kingswear to Newton Abbot on 2 June 1961. The GWR was the first of Britain's 'Big Four' to make any significant use of the diesel railcar on some cross-country and rural routes.
*P. W. Gray*

Exactly one year after the first of the class entered traffic, No D806 *Cambrian* is seen with the 7.30am Penzance to Manchester at Teignmouth on 14 July 1959. The first three members of this class were a belated addition to BR's Pilot Scheme orders; and whilst the design was entirely due to German engineering skill, No D800 was constructed almost entirely by hand, the staff at Swindon having to translate specifications into a design that would fit the British loading gauge. *R. C. Riley*

*Above:*
This picture, taken on 1 July 1964, shows an unidentified 'Hymek' B-B as it crosses the now demolished bridge into Barnstaple with a train from Ilfracombe. Today the terminus of the 'Tarka Line' from Exeter, Barnstaple was once the hub of an intricate pattern of services to the coastal resorts of North Devon and Cornwall. *John Edgington*

*Below:*
Another view of Barnstaple, this time the driver of 'Warship' No D826 *Jupiter* prepares to hand over the single-line token as he enters with an Ilfracombe to Paddington train in 1967. In addition to the lines to Ilfracombe and Exeter, other lines radiating from Barnstaple were the lines to Taunton and to Halwill Junction. *Mike Squires*

An excellent portrait of 1,750hp English Electric Co Type 3 Co-Co No D6934 as it is seen between duties at Pantyffynon sub-shed on 23 June 1968. The locomotive has been fitted with a headlight for working the former LNWR Central Wales line between Craven Arms and Swansea. *K. Fairey*

*Above:*
**One of eight English Electric Type 3s transferred to Landore in August 1963, No D6853 is seen on the 15th of that month entering Fishguard with container traffic for the harbour.** *Derrick Codling*

*Below:*
**Single-unit railcar No W55019 waits to depart from Penarth on 8 July 1967 as the 12.05 shuttle service to Cadoxton.** *Hugh Ballantyne*

*Above:*
**Brush/Sulzer Type 4 No D1662 *Isambard Kingdom Brunel* passes North Somerset Junction semaphore signals with 1O61 — the 12.36 Cardiff to Portsmouth in April 1965. No D1662 had been named only one month earlier at Bristol Temple Meads station on Saturday 20 March by the Lord Mayor of Bristol, Councillor K. Dalby.** *Terry Nicholls*

*Below:*
**Another view taken in Bristol, this time depicting Beyer Peacock 'Hymek' No D7096 as it approaches Dr Days Bridge Junction with the 14.35 Cardiff to Bristol on 4 July 1969. Operating on numerous cross-country routes the 'Hymeks' fulfilled their role handling many of the duties formerly entrusted to the GWR 'Castles'.** *Hugh Ballantyne*

*Above:*
**The tranquil peace of the Forest of Dean is broken by North British Locomotive Co diesel-hydraulic No D6319 as it shunts Marsh Sidings at Parkend on 10 June 1968. In 1970 this 3½ mile branch from Lydney Junction came under threat of closure and the Dean Forest Railway Society was formed to operate it as a tourist railway.**
*W. Potter/N. Fields collection*

*Below:*
**Also in the Forest of Dean is BR Swindon 650hp diesel-hydraulic 0-6-0 No D9521 as it passes Dudbridge with the thrice-weekly goods from Gloucester to Stroud and Nailsworth on 4 March 1966. The type was designed for shunting and trip working, although much of this had disappeared before the first engine appeared in 1964.** *Hugh Ballantyne*

*Left:*
Awaiting acceptance trials outside 'A' shop at Swindon Works in May 1962 are North British Locomotive Co 1,000/1,100hp B-B diesel-hydraulics Nos D6343/D6341. This class, which eventually ran to 58 members, was more at home on secondary duties and local freight work, but with the closure of so many branch lines in the West Country, they became too numerous to retain in one area and were later to be seen all over WR territory. *T. B. Owen*

*Left:*
Seen carrying the darker two-tone green livery is the Brush-Maybach 2,800hp Co-Co prototype *Falcon* outside Swindon Works in April 1966. The locomotive had been repainted into BR green livery in August 1964 upon completion of its original test period.
*J. B. Hall/Colour-Rail (DE1881)*

*Below:*
Swiss-built Brown-Boveri A1A-A1A gas-turbine electric locomotive No 18000 receives attention outside Swindon Works on 18 May 1957. Duties for No 18000 in April 1957 included the down 'Merchant Venturer' the locomotive returning with the lightly loaded 4.15pm from Bristol. The formation of the 'Merchant Venturer' was of chocolate and cream stock which entered service on 1 April that year.
*T. B. Owen*

Carrying its original maroon livery, No D1001 *Western Pathfinder* stands outside Swindon Works in May 1963. One of 14 members of the class to carry this livery, the locomotive finally received the BR corporate blue livery with full yellow ends in November 1970. *Derek Penney*

*Top:*
Standing outside the stock shed at Swindon Works on 25 October 1964 is Beyer Peacock 'Hymek' No D7041. The demise of this class began with the introduction of BR's Rationalisation Policy, many of the class being withdrawn in 1972, although a few survivors lingered on in traffic until 1975. Behind is a Pressed Steel Class 117 DMU. *J. G. Dewing*

*Above:*
A familiar view in Sonning Cutting taken on 11 May 1963 as 'Warship' No D861 *Vigilant* heads an up parcels train for the London area. Careful observers will note that the third vehicle in the formation is an insulated cream van. *Neville Simms*

*Above:*
**Shortly after members of this class had been allocated to certain South Wales services, an unidentified 'Hymek' is seen passing the MPD at Southall with the down 'Red Dragon' in 1961.** *Cliff Woodhead*

*Below:*
**Still carrying its original colour scheme 'Warship' No D849 *Superb* passes the arrival signalbox at Paddington on Friday 6 July 1962 after arriving with an earlier train.** *Geoff Rixon*

*Right:*
Contrasting with experiences on the Continent the railbus experiment in Britain was a failure and the type was extinct by 1968. This photograph shows AC Cars four-wheel railbus W79977 at Kemble on 25 May 1963 as it prepares to return to Tetbury. The creditable experiment was not notably successful and the branch closed entirely from 6 April 1964. *Bryan Hicks*

*Above:*
Brush/Sulzer 2,750hp Co-Co diesel electric No D1588 is seen half a mile south of Stokesay Castle as it works the 12.55pm Manchester (Piccadilly) to Plymouth on 10 April 1965. The first member of the class, No D1500, had made its debut on 6 September 1962, when it travelled from Loughborough to Crewe for weighing. *M. Mensing*

*Left:*
This view taken at Worcester Shrub Hill on 2 June 1963 shows 'Hymek' No D7076 waiting for departure with a service from Paddington to Hereford. The original attractive Brunswick green livery was always pleasing to the eye with a grey roof, red buffer beams and lime green stripes at the body base. *R. C. Riley*

*Above:*
One of the second series of GWR railcars, No W32W, stands outside Worcester Works on 10 June 1956. In post-war years some cross-country routes operated by the diesels were Oxford-Worcester-Hereford, Reading-Newbury, Bristol-Weymouth and Gloucester-Birmingham. Branches served included Worcester-Bewdley and Gloucester-Ledbury. *N. Fields*

*Below:*
A classic study of a fine locomotive as 'Western' No D1002 *Western Explorer* breasts the summit of Hatton Bank with a down working in 1962. *Western Explorer* was released to traffic in green livery with small yellow panels — a first for Swindon as neither of the original two engines had received this treatment. *D. Penney*

With Corfe Castle prominent in the background, Birmingham Railway Carriage & Wagon Co 1,550hp Bo-Bo Type 3 No D6535 heads the 10.30 Waterloo to Swanage on 7 August 1965. Thanks to the preservation movement much of the branch from Worgret Junction to Swanage is still in existence. *Peter W. Gray*

# TWO

# Southern Region

A postwar priority for the Southern Railway was to continue its electrification programme in south-east England. General Manager Sir Eustace Missenden announced a £15 million programme on 31 October 1946 that would convert 284 route miles to electric working.

When the Modernisation Plan was announced in 1955, the Southern Region (SR) had already tried out six diesels (Bulleid-designed 1Co-Co1 Nos 10201/2/3 and three from the LMR, Co-Cos Nos 10000/1 and Bo-Bo No 10800).

By late January 1959 BR/Sulzer Bo-Bo Type 2 No D5000 was the first of 15 members of the class to be loaned to the Southern Region where it was used for crew training between Ashford and Faversham. Each locomotive weighed some five tons more than expected, and the civil engineer vetoed their use over certain sections. In order to overcome this problem, some locomotives had their train-heating boilers removed. This meant that there became two distinct groups of locomotives, D5002-6 and D5000/1/7-14, the latter having greater freedom of route availibility.

The weight of most of the early diesels gave rise to another problem, the lack of braking force availability. This became obvious on 10 November 1959; D5000, hauling a coal train from Snowdown colliery, ran through Snowdown station out of control, ploughed through a sand drag, demolished buffer stops, and finally came to rest on the side of a low cutting, fouling the up main line.

The Southern Region policy to eliminate steam traction area by area still left the SR with a need for a medium-powered diesel-electric locomotive to work some passenger and freight services over routes not scheduled for electrification.

In 1957 the BTC (British Transport Commission) had finalised five power ranges (Types 1-5) for the classification of the building of diesel locomotives. The standard medium-powered Type 3 favoured by the BTC was a Co-Co locomotive of 1,750hp designed by English Electric with a 12-cylinder vee engine.

However, the demands of the SR differed from the rest of the BR regions and its engineers had put forward their own proposal. Their calculations showed that a Bo-Bo locomotive developing 1,000-1,200hp would be sufficient to meet their needs. These could be summarised as follows:

i) The haulage of 700-ton freight trains on ruling gradients of 1 in 70.
ii) The haulage of 375-ton passenger and van trains to normal schedules.
iii) The capability to heat them by electricity.
iv) The capability to haul electric multiple-unit trains at normal speed over all routes in an emergency.
v) The ability to work vacuum and air braked stock.
vi) A maximum service speed of 85mph.
vii) The widest possible route availability.

A Sulzer proposal for a Bo-Bo locomotive was not accepted by British Railways but it interested the Southern Region engineers. A tender was later received from the Birmingham Railway Carriage & Wagon Company (BRCW) of Smethwick for a 76-ton Bo-Bo locomotive based on its 1,160/1,250hp Type 2. This proposal met the specification and in December 1957, the BRCW Type 3 (later Class 33) was put into production.

After the introduction of the BRCW Type 3s, the LM Type 2s were retained on the SR for a period to provide train heating, as the SR did not then have any electrically heated stock. Instead of using a steam train heating boiler, the locomotives were fitted with electrical train heating; the few winter diagrams intended for these engines meant that only a small number of coaches needed conversion to electrical heating.

Renumbered Class 33 under the TOPS system, 19 locomotives of this class were modified for remote control in 1966/7. At this time electrification from Waterloo had reached Bournemouth, but the section through to Weymouth posed a problem.

This was solved by using a mix of four-car units between Waterloo and Bournemouth, where one or two of the trailer units were worked forward to Weymouth by a Class 33. The same locomotive propelled its train back to Bournemouth under the control of the driver in the leading cab of the trailer unit.

*Top:*
**Transferred from the London Midland Region to the Southern Region together with sister locomotive No 10001 in March 1953, LMS pioneer main line diesel locomotive No 10000 heads the down 'Royal Wessex' near Shawford Junction in 1954.** *B. J. Swain/Colour-Rail (DE625)*

*Above:*
**Captured at Three Bridges in March 1963 is one of the three Southern Railway booster locomotives, No 20002. All three booster locomotives carried two booster sets, each supplying three of the traction motors and coupled to a blower for traction motor cooling.** *Geoff Rixon*

*Top:*
**Seen with an up train in Dorchester South up bay in May 1952 is one of the SR/English Electric Co prototypes, No 10201.With SR loading gauge and civil engineering restrictions it was built with a 1Co-Co1 wheel arrangement.** *S. C. Townroe/Colour-Rail (DE628)*

*Above:*
**A superb portrait of sister locomotive No 10203 as it stands outside Eastleigh Works in 1954. Nos 10201/2 were transferred to the LMR in April 1955 and were followed by No 10203 after some more test runs on the Southern.** *B. J. Swain/Colour-Rail (DE1512)*

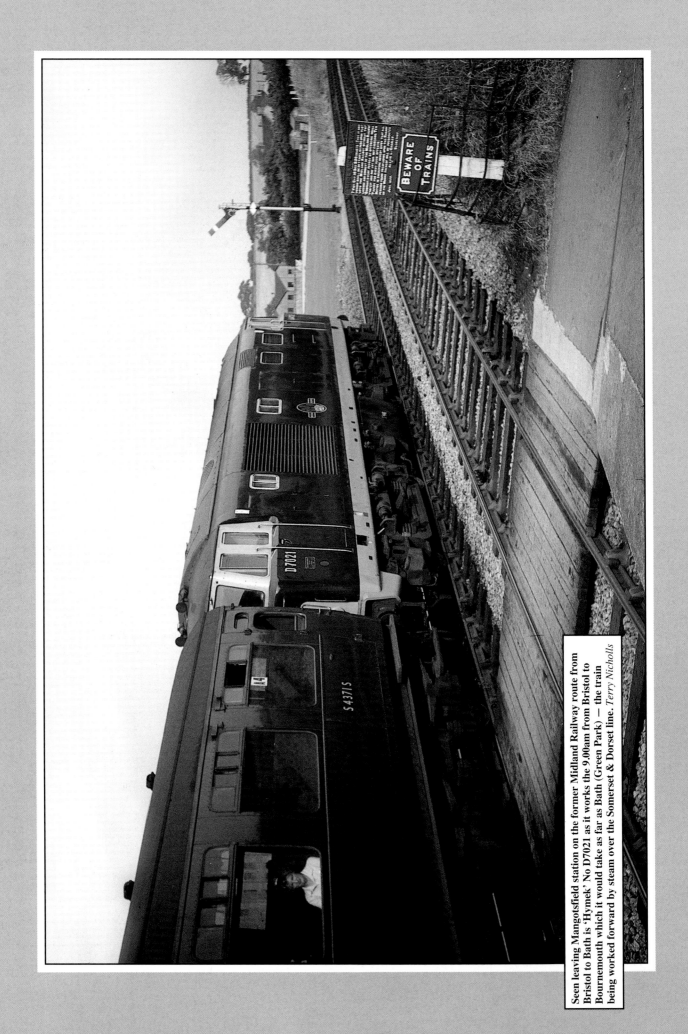

Seen leaving Mangotsfield station on the former Midland Railway route from Bristol to Bath is 'Hymek' No D7021 as it works the 9.00am from Bristol to Bournemouth which it would take as far as Bath (Green Park) — the train being worked forward by steam over the Somerset & Dorset line. *Terry Nicholls*

*Above:*

A popular vantage point for photographers wishing to see locomotives climbing the final mile of 1 in 50 past Upwey Wishing Well Halt up to Bincombe Tunnel. Here this view sees 'Hymek' No D7013 working a Weymouth to Wolverhampton train. The 101 'Hymeks' (originally 301 were once projected) were logical developments of the underpowered Type 2s of the early modernisation era. The class was condemned between September 1971 and March 1975 (No D7013 in January 1972), victims of BTC 'central planning'. *Derek Cross*

*Left:*

A somewhat shabby Class 120 DMU is seen leaving Templecombe station on 5 March 1966. In 1966, 22 sets were transferred from the WR to Derby, to replace the less successful Cravens and BRCW units. *Gavin Morrison*

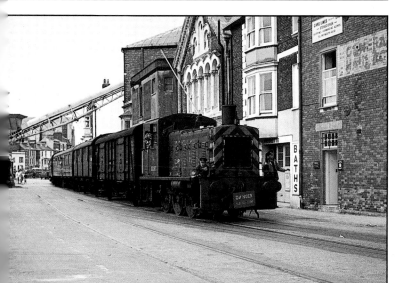

*Left:*

In only the second week of diesel shunter haulage on Weymouth Quay, No D2397 heads a Waterloo to Channel Islands boat train in July 1964. The first diesel shunter to be allocated to Weymouth was on 5 December 1961, from which date a 204hp diesel-mechanical worked on Duty 457 in the Town goods yard. The short tramway to Weymouth Quay, just over a mile long, was opened in 1865 and from 1889 Channel Islands boat trains began to make their way through the streets. *John Edgington*

*Above:*
**Brush/Sulzer 2,750hp Co-Co diesel-electric No D1967 has charge of the southbound 'Pines Express' approaching <u>Sway</u>, west of Brockenhurst, on 10 September 1966. At that time some of the SR's Brush Type 4s found use on Bournemouth expresses, including the 'Bournemouth Belle' Pullman train, but otherwise steam reigned supreme on what became Britain's last steam-worked passenger main line.** *M. Mensing*

NEW MILTON

*Left:*
**Beyer Peacock 'Hymek' No D7015 is seen near Branksome on 31 August 1965, the 8C27 headcode panel being incorrect for this working. It was only four years earlier that the first member of the class had been handed over to BR's Western Region officials at a ceremony at Paddington on 16 May 1961, the locomotive entering revenue-earning service in the Bristol area in the week commencing 10 July 1961.** *Gavin Morrison*

*Above:*
This May 1967 picture taken near Brockenhurst sees Brush/Sulzer Type 4 No D1921 in charge of the down 'Bournemouth Belle'. Conductor rails have been laid in preparation for the switch-on of third rail electrification.

*Below:*
Primroses are in evidence as BRCW Co 1,550hp Bo-Bo Type 3 No D6501 heads a westbound permanent way train carrying concrete sleepers in the New Forest near Brockenhurst, also in May 1967.
*Both: Derek Cross*

*Right:*
BRCW Type 3 No D6549 heads a down express near Micheldever on 29 May 1967. Later that year, on Sunday 10 September, No D6549 had the unenviable task of hauling away the last of the Bulleid Pacifics from Nine Elms. The locomotives in question being 'Merchant Navy' No 35023 *Holland-Afrika Line* and 'Battle of Britain' No 34084 *253 Squadron*. *Bryan Hicks*

*Above:*
In this picture BRCW Type 3 No D6522 is seen near Lyndhurst Road on 18 June 1967 with a train comprised of unpowered TC units, which were converted from Mk 1 coaches. The leading 3TC set would be strengthened to four vehicles in 1974. *Peter Fitton*

*Left:*
Hither Green Civil Engineers' Department 1948 Drewry 0-6-0 No DS1173 is pictured at Eastleigh on 11 September 1960. *John Edgington*

*Above:*

**BR Corporate Blue liveried Mk 1 rolling stock is well in evidence in this July 1967 picture of 'Hymek' No D7060 as it heads a down train in the New Forest near Beaulieu Road. Two months later, in September 1967, six members of the class were re-allocated to Worcester, of which three were to be kept at Bromsgrove at any one time for banking duties on the Lickey Incline. The remainder were used for local workings from Worcester and worked turn and turn about with those at Bromsgrove.**
*Derek Penney*

*Right:*

**Carefully framed in the pine trees, a two-car diesel-electric unit speeds a Southampton to Lymington service east of Brockenhurst in May 1967.**
*Derek Cross*

*Top:*

**Although the WR's 'Western' class diesel hydraulics were more highly regarded by enthusiasts, the B-B 'Warships' of 2,200hp put in some hard work on the Western Region (and on some Southern Region lines). From 1964 'Warships' worked Waterloo to West of England expresses as seen in this view of D804 *Avenger* at Basingstoke on 14 August 1965.** *Ray Reed*

*Above:*

**A rare visitor to Southern Region metals is Brush Type 2 No D5666 at Farnborough with a special from the Eastern Region for the airshow on 9 September 1962. The train has just passed under a set of semi-automatic electro-pneumatic semaphores which were in operation from Woking almost to Basingstoke.** *Rodney Lissenden*

*Above:*
**This February 1967 picture depicts BRCW 1,550hp Bo-Bo Type 3 No D6509 with a down Bournemouth train passing under the semaphores at Byfleet Junction.**

*Below:*
**Western Region 'Warship' No D806 *Cambrian* is seen on Southern Region metals passing Esher with a West of England to Waterloo express on 3 April 1965.** *Both: Geoff Rixon*

*Top:*
**Brush/Sulzer 2,750hp Co-Co Type 4 No D1921 approaches Esher station in November 1966 with an empty coaching stock special for Eastleigh Works.** *Geoff Rixon*

*Above:*
**This powerful October 1966 image shows doyen of the class, 'Warship' No D800** *Sir Brian Robertson***, as it approaches Vauxhall station with a Waterloo to West of England express.** *Ray Reed*

*Top:*
**This 21 April 1963 picture shows BRCW Co Type 3 No D6567 sharing facilities with steam locomotives at Three Bridges MPD. The first of an order of 98 locomotives of this class had arrived at Hither Green from BRCW Co on 17 December 1959.** *Ray Reed*

*Above:*
**A rare picture of diesel-electric 0-6-0 No D3044 working a test train formed mainly of loaded coal wagons on the former East Kent Railway past Tilmanstone Colliery near Eythorne station.** *Derek Cross*

*Above:*
Some six months after the first of the class had arrived on the Southern region, BRCW Bo-Bo Type 3 No D6502 stands in the carriage sidings at Folkestone Junction on 5 June 1960. Primarily designed for use on freight traffic, the type basically followed that of the BRCW 'D5300' class. *Rodney Lissenden*

*Below:*
Itinerant BRCW Bo-Bo Type 3 No D6538 (73C) has arrived at Coventry on 28 May 1963 with an excursion from Margate to the then new cathedral. Another excursion to Coventry the next day brought sister locomotive No D6549 (73C) from Portsmouth. *Ray Reed*

Before the tranquillity of the Lune Gorge near Tebay was permanently shattered by the arrival of the M6 motorway, the autumn tints of the moors complement the two-tone livery of Brush/Sulzer Type 4 No D1524 as it works a southbound tube train over Dillicar troughs. *Derek Huntriss*

# THREE

# London Midland Region

After pioneering the development of the diesel locomotive for 15 years from the 1930s with its 350/400hp diesel shunters, the London, Midland & Scottish Railway was the first British company to introduce main-line diesel-electric traction in the form of two units, Nos 10000 and 10001. No 10000 was completed at Derby Works in early December 1947. After 10 days of extensive tests and trial runs, it was despatched to London for inspection by the directors. Together with new Stanier Pacific No 6256 it was on show at Euston on 18 December and subsequently took a test train to Watford and back.

No 10001 was completed six months after Nationalisation and the pair made their debut on the West Coast main line on 7 October 1948, hauling the 11.40pm Euston to Glasgow sleeping car train as far as Carlisle. On 1 June 1949 the pair made a demonstration run with the down 'Royal Scot', arriving three minutes early at Glasgow Central and receiving the kind of welcome usually reserved for film stars, the crew posing for photographs and signing countless autograph books. However, steam traction made its reply when No 46225 *Duchess of Gloucester* arrived at an adjacent platform also three minutes early, with the 10.10am ex Euston.

The London Midland Region was the first to receive new motive power under the 1955 Modernisation Plan on receipt of English Electric Bo-Bo Type 1 No D8000. The 'D8000' class outlived most of its contemporaries, its success lying with the design which incorporated well-proven equipment. Considerable effort was made to produce an attractive piece of industrial design, No D8000 being formally handed over to the BTC on 3 June 1957.

The first 20 of the class were allocated to Devons Road motive power depot, the first steam depot in the country to be completely converted for the maintenance of diesel locomotives. However, the life of Devons Road was to be relatively short; closed from 10 February 1964, its duties were divided between Stratford and Willesden.

It wasn't until 1958 that the first British Railways home-grown diesel design emerged from Derby Works in the form of No D5000, a relatively lightweight double-cab Bo-Bo locomotive, carrying a Sulzer six-cylinder in-line slow speed engine supplying 1,160hp through BTH equipment. With a top speed of 75mph and weighing 75 tons, the BR/Sulzer Type 2s were a lightweight mixed traffic class.

However, when the English Electric Type 4s were introduced on the West Coast main as an interim measure before electrification of the route was complete, they shared the facilities of Camden depot with their steam counterparts, although in later years some new depot building took place at Carlisle Kingmoor, Toton and Cricklewood.

On the Midland lines out of St Pancras, The 'Peak' BR/Sulzer Type 4s were concentrated on all main line trains. A comprehensive, regular interval timetable was introduced with interconnecting trains for Sheffield hourly, alternately via Derby and Nottingham with semi-fast trains feeding into each at Leicester. The 'Peaks' reliably achieved running speeds of 90mph and were equally at home on freight workings although the heavy Toton to Brent coal workings were usually entrusted to pairs of Type 2s. The dieselisation of the Manchester services was virtually complete by February 1961 and led to a marked improvement in timekeeping. The 'Peaks' were regular performers on the cross-country services from north-east to south-west, being the first diesel-electrics to be received by the Western Region, penetrating the diesel-hydraulic strongholds of Devon and Cornwall and dominating these duties until the introduction of the Inter-City 125 units in 1983.

The pressure to improve the public image of passenger services meant that the replacement of steam traction on freight duties was left until last. Having witnessed the unsuccessful performance of the Clayton Type 1s in Scotland, the London Midland Region ordered large numbers of BR/Sulzer Type 2s and English Electric Type 1s which were delivered at about the same time as the Beeching route closures came into effect. At this time the opportunity was taken to rid the railway of the least successful locomotives and DMUs. The Metrovick / Crossley Co-Bos were scrapped, as were many of the early 'Derby Lightweight' DMUs — some Type 2s being displaced to the Western Region.

47

*Top:*
**In this panoramic view of Carlisle Kingmoor (12A) MPD taken on 4 June 1965, an unidentified English Electric Co 2,000hp 1Co-Co1 Type 4 passes with an up passenger working.** *M. S. Welch*

*Above:*
**Always associated with their duties on the Midland main line, BR/Sulzer 'Peak' Type 4 No D16 has arrived at Carlisle with the up 'Waverley' on 19 August 1967.** *Ray Reed*

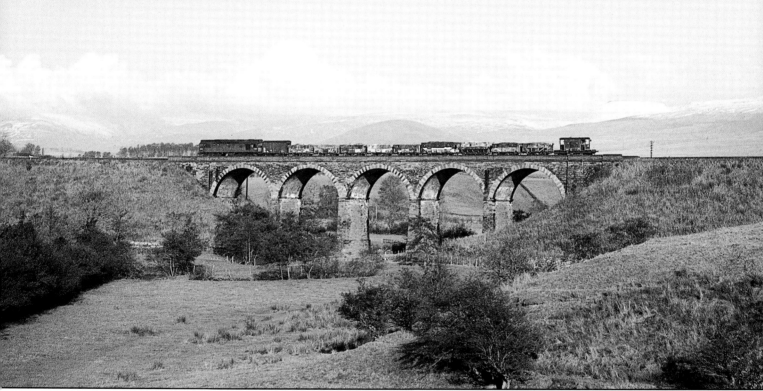

*Above:*
**Showing signs of recent fire damage, BR/Sulzer Type 2 No D7516 is seen passing the closed station at Cumwhinton with a southbound freight over the Settle & Carlisle in July 1971.** *Geoff Greenwood*

*Below:*
**Another view of a BR/Sulzer Type 2 at work on the Settle & Carlisle route, this time No D7508 is at the head of a down freight as it passes over Long Marton viaduct on 8 November 1967. Eventually a total of 477 BR/Sulzer Type 2s was constructed, the first 151 members of the class being designated Class 24 and the remainder Class 25.** *Neville Simms*

Another autumnal view taken in the Lune Gorge south of Tebay on 4 November 1967. This time English Electric Type 4 No D283 is seen working a southbound fitted freight. At that time the photographer was cursing that these trains were not steam hauled in such beautiful weather conditions, but time has tempered his judgement. *Derek Huntriss*

Another day of dramatic lighting in the northern fells. Here BR Class 25 No D5194 gets the right of way from the up loop at Grayrigg with a short permanent way train from a former London & North Western Railway lower quadrant semaphore on 18 July 1971. Of the 477 BR/Sulzer Type 2 locomotives constructed it was sister engine No D7667 that held the honour of being the 1,000th diesel locomotive built at Derby. *Peter Fitton*

Top:
The northern fells can also produce some of the worst weather known to man, as can be seen in this picture taken on the Settle & Carlisle line at Blea Moor on 15 February 1969 as English Electric Type 4 No D208 emerges from the tunnel with a freight consisting of empty steel plate wagons. *F. Bullock*

Above:
Against a backdrop of a snow-covered Pen-y-Ghent BR/Sulzer Class 24 No 5097 passes Selside village north of Horton in Ribblesdale towards Blea Moor with a loaded coal train on 29 November 1969. Early members of this class had weight restriction problems which were overcome by removing their train heating boilers. *Gavin Morrison*

52

*Above:*
**In this 5 June 1964 picture Barrow MPD's Metropolitan-Vickers 1,200hp Co-Bo No D5714 is passing Carnforth with the 18.50 Heysham Moss to Whitehaven Fina tank train.** *Derrick Codling*

*Below:*
**This Trans-Pennine DMU seen at Keswick on 30 August 1964 had originated from Leeds and travelled via Colne and Ravenglass, the return working being via Workington, Penrith and Ingleton.** *Derrick Codling*

*Right:*
Seen in a line of new locomotives standing at Rugby on their way to an exhibition at Willesden in 1954 is the BR/Paxman/Fell 2,040hp DM 4-4-4-4 No 10100. Originally constructed as a 2-D-2, No 10100 was outshopped from Derby Works in May 1952. The 4ft 3in coupled wheels were driven through gearing calculated to give a top speed of 78mph when the four main engines were running at their maximum speed of 1,500rpm. *J. M. Jarvis/Colour-Rail (DE1657)*

*Above:*
This May 1968 view portrays the Brush/Sulzer 3,946hp Co-Co prototype *Kestrel* outside Crewe Works. Design consultants Wilkes & Ashmore had advised on the outward appearance, giving the cabs a more streamlined form with a view towards high speed operation. The livery chosen for *Kestrel* was a striking combination of grey roof, golden yellow body above the waistline and chocolate brown below. *M. Burnett/Colour-Rail (DE695)*

*Left:*
In this 1965 picture when Euston station was being rebuilt and sister LMS/English Electric Co-Co prototype No 10000 had already been withdrawn in December 1963, No 10001 is relegated to empty carriage stock (ecs) working to Willesden. *John Edgington*

54

*Above:*
**The English-Electric Co 2,700hp prototype No DP2 takes the up fast line through Tring cutting in May 1963. After covering over 100,000 miles in traffic No DP2 was generally considered to be the most successful diesel-electric to be operating in Britain.** *T. B. Owen*

*Below:*
**The prototype No GT3 stands in Vulcan Works yard, Newton-le-Willows, in September 1963. The GT3 was a 4-6-0 locomotive of similar size to the BR Standard Class 5. Its general appearance, together with the unusual brown livery, inspired a certain aesthetic satisfaction.**
*A. Wild/Colour-Rail (DE1409)*

*Above:*
A civil engineering picture showing modifications to Bridge 5 during the A34 road widening scheme near Stone on 18 August 1959, also depicts a Birmingham Railway Carriage & Wagon Co three-car DMU passing with a down service. This particularly useful type was introduced in 1957 for branch line and general local services. *M. S. Welch*

*Below:*
A two-car DMU forms a local service to Birkenhead in this picture taken at Helsby on 25 April 1964. This line was operated as a GWR/LNWR joint operation, the line behind the station building being that from Chester to Warrington. *Peter Fitton*

*Left:*
**BR/Sulzer Bo-Bo Type 2 No D7608 has charge of a Sheffield to Chinley local on the former Midland Railway Dore & Chinley line near Edale on 9 July 1966. The Class 25 as the type became under TOPS did not prove to be BR's best design of Type 2 and its survival probably owed much to its numerical size — the weak feature of the type being the traction motors which must have proved costly to maintain.**
*Bryan Hicks*

*Left:*
**BR/Sulzer Production series 'Peak' 1Co-Co1 diesel-electric No D113 pilots BR/Sulzer 1,250hp Bo-Bo Type 2 No D5267 with the 17.18 Sheffield (Midland) to Manchester (Central) past Chinley East Junction on Whit Sunday, 17 May 1964.** *M. Mensing*

*Below:*
**An empty mgr train is seen arriving at Shirebrook Colliery bunker in June 1968 behind Brush/Sulzer 2,650hp Co-Co Type 4 No D1899.**
*Cliff Woodhead*

An interesting picture taken inside Derby Works on 12 April 1959 as both the first 'Peak', No D1 *Scafell Pike*, and BR/Sulzer Type 2 No D5015 near completion. No D1, the first of the ten pilot scheme 'Peaks', travelled up to London for inspection on 21 April and was officially named *Scafell Pike* by Sir Fergus Graham, Lord Lieutenant of Cumberland at a ceremony at Carlisle Citadel station on 14 July 1959. *T. B. Owen*

*Above:*
**In this tranquil setting at Betws-y-Coed a two-car 'Derby Heavyweight' unit (later Class 108) departs for Blaenau Ffestiniog. Today, this scenic line which runs from Llandudno Junction to Blaenau Ffestiniog is promoted as the Conwy Valley Line.** *Derek Cross*

*Below:*
**BR/Sulzer 'Peak' No D104 passes Gowhole yard with a Manchester Central to St Pancras train on 10 September 1966. Today, reductions in traffic and improvements in motive power have once again seen a return to a straightforward double-track layout, the two lines farthest from the camera having been removed.** *Dr L. A. Nixon*

**Even to the most broad-minded observer of new diesel locomotives, the appearance of the 1,200hp Metropolitan-Vickers Co-Bos must have been distinctly odd, with their different bogies, one six-wheel and one four-wheel, and unusual livery scheme, various parts being picked out in duck-egg blue. Here, No D5702 is under test outside the Paint Shop at Crewe Works on 31 March 1963.** *Ray Reed*

**With the radio masts at Droitwich visible in the background, 'Peak' No D33 works unassisted past Vigo on the Lickey Incline with an 11-coach train for Bradford on 18 August 1962.** *T. B. Owen*

**Diverted off the Stour Valley line for electrification works, English Electric Type 4 No D318 is approaching Hilltop Tunnel on the WR Birmingham to Wolverhampton route on what was nominally the 17.25 Birmingham (Snow Hill) to Liverpool (Lime Street) and Manchester (Piccadilly) on Sunday 24 April 1966. But for the diversion this train would have been operated out of Birmingham (New Street).** *M. Mensing*

*Below:*
**One of Sheffield Darnall's allocation of English Electric Co-Co Type 3s awaits departure from Nottingham Victoria with the 10.00 York to Bournemouth (West) in March 1966.** *Colour-Rail*

*Bottom:*
**On the occasion of the Queen's visit to the Royal Show, totally immaculate English-Electric Type 4 No D371 stands in the rebuilt station at Coventry with the stock of the Royal Train on 4 July 1963.** *Ray Reed*

*Above:*
A two-car Park Royal DMU changes platforms on a frosty 2 January 1965 at Leamington Spa Avenue to form a service to Coventry and Nuneaton. This service was to be discontinued just two weeks later on 18th January when the line lost its passenger service. The first diesel train to serve Leamington was as early as March 1956 when diesels from Birmingham operated the line as a filling in turn. *Bryan Hicks*

*Below:*
Cravens Parcels Unit No M55998 is seen in the north bay at Rugby on 27 July 1963. Previously used for trains to Leamington and Leicester, the north bay platforms at Rugby are now closed to passengers and are used as a stabling point for locomotives. The three diesel parcels cars built by Cravens were introduced in August 1958. *H. W. Robinson/N. Simms collection*

*Top:*
**A Bakerloo Line train can be seen departing on the left of this picture taken in 1961 at Harrow & Wealdstone station as English Electric Type 4 No D220 heads an up train for Euston. Replacement signals on the down fast line were installed after the disaster of 8 October 1952.**
*Geoff Rixon*

*Above:*
**Prior to the introduction of yellow warning panels, an unidentified English Electric Type 4 is taking water from Bushey troughs whilst working an up train on 7 May 1960. This operation replenished the water in the locomotive's train heating boiler.** *T. B. Owen*

*Above:*
**The steam/diesel transition at Euston is clearly seen is this picture taken of arrival Platforms 1 and 2 in August 1962 as LMS Pacific No 46252 *City of Leicester* stands alongside English Electric Type 4 No D380.** *Geoff Rixon*

*Below:*
**Another view at Euston, this time taken in 1963, sees an unidentified English Electric Type 4 having just arrived at platform 2 with the 'Emerald Isle Express'.** *M. S. Welch*

A superb detail portrait of a magnificent machine. This 1962 picture shows 'Deltic' No D9012 *Crepello* heading north from Grantham with 1N16, the 12:45pm King's Cross to Leeds. *Crepello* had entered traffic on 12 September 1961, the next day it worked the down 'Yorkshire Pullman'. *Derek Penney*

# FOUR

# Eastern Region

It was the Western Region that was first to eliminate all steam traction from its routes but the Eastern had managed to achieve BR's first steam-free division. With its main line trains from Liverpool Street to Cambridge and Norwich having nothing more than the Gresley 'B2' and 'B17' 4-6-0s, dieselisation was concentrated in East Anglia with English Electric Type 4s taking over the top expresses and Brush Type 2s working the remaining principal services and DMUs taking over the branch line work. Unlike other Regions, the ER decided not to adapt existing steam depots but to construct purpose-built depots wherever possible.

The East Coast main line pioneered some of the first English Electric Type 4s which found use on some of the principal trains including the 'Flying Scotsman'. However, it was to be another class of diesel that would become the pride of the East Coast main line — the English Electric Co 3,300hp Type 5 'Deltic'. After undergoing trials on the LMR, with the pending electrification of the West Coast main line it was obvious that the future of the prototype *Deltic* lay elsewhere and it was transferred to York on 13 January 1956 for trials on the North Eastern Region (NER). After two days of tests it ventured as far as Marshalls Meadow (Berwick) with a six-wheeled saloon on 16 January. It proved to be slightly out of gauge, losing its cab steps at Darlington and dislodging a section of the platform edge at Newcastle (Manors). By the end of that month it had been transferred to Hornsey for trials on the Great Northern (GNR) lines. Unfortunately it failed on arrival and was returned to works for a replacement No 1 power unit. Non-stop trials commenced on 16 March 1958 but had to be terminated at Gateshead (Greenfield) due to limited clearance at Newcastle Central. The journey was completed in 3 hours 45 minutes, some 15 minutes faster than the prewar 'Silver Jubilee' timing.

Due to the success of the prototype the British Transport Commission signed a contract with English Electric for the manufacture and full maintenance of 22 locomotives in March 1958. In this contract English Electric guaranteed that each locomotive would cover an average of 205,000 miles per annum — a distance some four times greater than the annual mileage of each Gresley 'A4' Pacific. With the ability to cut 40 minutes off the journey between King's Cross and Darlington, the effect on East Coast main line services was dramatic. The first locomotive to arrive at Doncaster for trials had been No D9001 on 17 January 1961, a corner of the works being set aside for stabling prior to allocation to permanent quarters on the East Coast route. On its second trial trip, No D9001 touched 100mph down Stoke Bank with a load of 14 bogies.

A system of double section block working was introduced for trials in the up direction, with the same bell signal, four-pause-four, which was used for the 'Silver Jubilee' and 'Coronation' workings before World War 2. At the same time, existing distant signals were converted from semaphore to colour light, and set back pending the introduction of the new timetable when all of the 'Deltics' were to enter traffic.

In 1969 BR took over responsibility for the maintenance programme of the 'Deltics' from English Electric. Unfortunately by 1971 serious problems were being encountered with the engines and crisis point was reached when over half of the class were out of action and unfit for traffic. With the advent of the 'InterCity 125' on the East Coast main line the days of the 'Deltic' were numbered. The class was utilised on easier duties but the first locomotive was withdrawn in 1980, the last one pulling out of Kings Cross on 2 January 1982.

For over 20 years, the 'Deltics' achieved a very high utilisation on the East Coast route, being at the forefront of diesel electric traction. Like the 'A3s' and 'A4s' before them, the 'Deltics' attracted a cult following with no fewer than six examples being preserved, in addition to the prototype.

One side-effect of the policy giving priority to the dieselisation of passenger and main line freight sevices was the creation of pockets of steam working where some of the oldest locomotives in BR's fleet were still at work. In the Tyne-Tees area ex-NER Class Q6 and J27s survived until 1967 when their replacements were the last deliveries of English Electric Type 3s, BR/Sulzer Type 2s and Clayton Type 1s. The fact that these ageing steam engines survived in traffic so long is a credit to their design.

*Right:*
**After working acceptance trials from Doncaster, production series North British Locomotive Co (NBL) Type 2 No D6114 is pictured outside Stratford Works on 2 June 1959. The first batch of 10 locomotives (D6100-9) were built as part of BR's pilot scheme and were initially allocated to Hornsey for use on GN line suburban duties.** *R. C. Riley*

*Above:*
**Following delivery to the Eastern Region, North British Locomotive Co 800hp No D8406 is seen at Stratford (30A) MPD on 3 June 1959. The design of the 10 pilot scheme Type A (later Type 1) 800hp locomotives closely resembled the stark appearance of the pioneer LMSR Bo-Bo No 10800 which NBL had built in 1950. Outwardly they were austere although some effort had been made to improve the design of the cab by placing the doors in the sides instead of at the ends.** *R. C. Riley*

*Right:*
**A line up of English Electric 'Baby Deltics' is seen outside Stratford MPD on 7 April 1963. By late April 1962, the availability of 'Baby Deltics' had reached a low ebb, only two being in traffic. As each engine failed it was withdrawn from traffic and stored, pending return to English Electric where an extensive refurbishing programme was put in hand.** *T. B. Owen*

*Top:*
**The production batches of Brush Type 2s were basically similar to the pilot scheme design, although the introduction of a four-panel route indicator altered their front end appearance. The two variations are depicted here at Stratford MPD on 27 February 1960. The locomotive on the left, No D5579, is carrying the experimental golden ochre livery.**
*M. S. Welch*

*Above:*
**English Electric Co-Co Type 3 No D6722 is seen approaching Chelmsford on 17 May 1964 with the 10.45 Norwich to Liverpool Street. By the end of February 1961, the early members of the class had been employed on dynamometer car trials on the Cambridge main line, the trains being formed of 25 to 38 'Minfits'.** *M. Mensing*

*Above:*
**English Electric Type 4 No D200 made its debut on the Great Eastern on 18 April 1958 when it worked a nine-coach train from Liverpool Street to Norwich with a head board announcing 'The first 2,000hp diesel run between Norwich and Liverpool Street'. Here it is seen on 24 April 1959 passing Stowmarket.** *Colour-Rail*

*Below:*
**Featured in this picture taken at Parkeston Quay MPD on 9 August 1965 is Brush Type 2 No D5576 and behind this locomotive is BTH Bo-Bo Type 1 No D8216. Also on shed that day was Departmental No 27 (formerly Class B1 4-6-0 No 61105) which was still in use for carriage heating purposes.** *Neville Simms*

71

*Below:*
**A timeless scene at Audley End in northwest Essex on the London to Cambridge main line as a pair of Brush Type 2s, Nos D5627 and D5693, power a freight through the station on 15 June 1963. Audley End was the junction for the branch to Saffron Walden.** *Colour-Rail*

*Bottom:*
**A Gresley Brake Third Corridor coach is immediately behind English Electric Type 3 No D6703 in this picture taken at Cambridge on 16 June 1962. Above the locomotive can be seen a fine array of early LNER signals.** *Colour-Rail*

*Above:*
**A Gresley Brake Composite and a Thompson postwar coach are in the formation of the 5.30pm King's Lynn to Liverpool Street as it leaves Ely behind Brush Type 2 No D5508 on Sunday, 19 July 1959.** *M. Mensing*

*Below:*
**A much later picture of a Brush Type 2 as No 5820 (minus the D prefix) with full yellow ends and corporate BR logo works the 13.30 Mablethorpe to Sheffield away from Boston on 11 July 1970.**
*Colour-Rail*

*Top:*
**This June 1959 picture sees the prototype *Deltic* working an up express on the GN main line away from the short tunnel at Askham. As early as December 1954, English Electric had decided to invest in the construction of its 3,300hp prototype. After success with the Napier engine in marine applications, English Electric planned a powerful express locomotive to meet BR needs.** *Peter Hughes/Colour-Rail (DE574)*

*Above:*
**Built as a private venture by a consortium which included Associated Electrical Industries, The Birmingham Railway Carriage & Wagon Co and Sulzer Bros (London) Ltd, the locomotive *Lion* was the first medium-speed-engine prototype to conform to BR's requirements for a second-generation Type 4 six-axle locomotive of at least 2,500hp. It is seen here leaving Sheffield with the up 'Sheffield Pullman'.** *Cliff Woodhead*

*Above:*
**Seen here departing from King's Cross in June 1962, the Brush/Maybach 2,800hp Co-Co prototype *Falcon* No D0280 had arrived at Finsbury Park depot on 13 June 1961. Its first duty in revenue-earning service came on 16 October when it worked the 6.52am King's Cross to Cambridge, returning at 10.05am.** *Geoff Rixon*

*Below:*
**'Baby Deltic' No D5900 is seen at the end of Platform No 15 at King's Cross in May 1965 after refurbishment at English Electric. Failures continued, however, and despite extensive modifications, the class did not escape BR's rationalisation plan, the last member, No D5909, being withdrawn in March 1971.** *F. Hornby/Colour-Rail (DE1250)*

*Right:* **Production version Brush Type 2 No D5679 emerges from Copenhagen Tunnel with an up local for King's Cross on 18 March 1961. It was on top of this tunnel that a house was constructed and used for the filming of the Ealing Comedy** *The Ladykillers. R. C. Riley*

*Above:*
**Brush Type 2 No D5679 is featured once again, this time hauling two sets of Gresley 'Quad-Arts' away from Hadley Wood with a northbound commuter train on 9 May 1963. The last link between the Great Northern Railway and Eastern Region King's Cross suburban services was broken in April 1966 when the last of Gresley's quad-art articulated suburban sets was withdrawn.** *Roy Hobbs*

*Left:*
**After returning from tests on the WR, Brush Type 4 No D1500 is depicted inside Finsbury Park depot in March 1963. On 2 November 1962 it had been transferred to Swindon for dynamometer car trials which included the moving of a 16-coach load from a dead stand on Dainton Bank.** *Roy Hobbs*

*Above:*
A classic study of a 'Deltic'-hauled Pullman train as D9007 *Pinza* passes Holloway South down signalbox with the 'Harrogate Sunday Pullman' on 9 June 1963. *Pinza* had entered traffic on 22 June 1961, its nameplate being fitted in Doncaster Works without ceremony. *Rodney Lissenden*

*Below:*
A Cravens two-car DMU (later Class 105) passes Brookmans Park on the Great Northern main line on 28 February 1959, bank fires from earlier steam-hauled trains being evident behind the unit. *T. B. Owen*

**English Electric Type 3 No D6740 is depicted on the Great Central main line at Leicester Central with an up Rugby League excursion on 9 May 1964. The York to Bournemouth workings over this route had been dieselised in September 1962 using Darnall Type 3s.** *R. C. Riley*

**With only two weeks to go before closure of this section of the former Great Central main line, a Derby-built four-car high-density DMU set is seen leaving Catesby Tunnel as a Nottingham Victoria to Marylebone service on 20 August 1966.** *Neville Simms*

*Above:*
This picture at Chapeltown sees Brush Type 2 No D5827 with a coal 'trip' working in spring 1967. The widespread introduction of yellow warning panels came after it was felt that the green livery blended into the general backcloth of the countryside and that with the locomotives relatively quiet operation they were a danger to permanent way staff.

*Below:*
With the trans-Pennine Woodhead route electric equipment very much in evidence, English Electric Type 3 No D6751 is seen departing from Sheffield Victoria on 28 February 1962 with the 12.41pm for Nottingham Victoria. *Both: Cliff Woodhead*

*Above:*
**A superb shot of English Electric Type 4 No D258 in action on the GN main line as it heads a southbound working up Gamston Bank near Retford in 1959. The first of the 10 pilot scheme locomotives to haul the prestigious 'Flying Scotsman' was No D209 on 31 January 1959.**

*Below:*
**Un-named 'Deltic' No D9017 heads a down express north of Grantham in 1962. Unlike a number of 'Deltics' No D9017 had a formal naming ceremony at Durham on 29 October 1963 when it was given the name *The Durham Light Infantry*.** *Both: Derek Penney*

*Left:*
Supplanted by 'Deltics' and Brush Type 4s on the ER and by Class 50s on the LMR, other than duties in Scotland the English Electric Type 4s were left with back up roles which included a substantial amount of freight workings. Here No D392 is passing Lockwood near Huddersfield with a freight working on 8 February 1967. *Gavin Morrison*

*Left:*
It is most unlikely that many of the passengers on this train would believe that they were travelling to work by Rolls-Royce. The Calder Valley DMUs (later Class 110) were powered by four 180hp Rolls-Royce diesel engines which ranked them amongst the most interesting DMUs on British Rail. This 1962 picture shows a three-car set emerging from Weasel Hall Tunnel near Hebden Bridge. *Geoff Greenwood*

*Below:*
Another English Electric Type 4 on freight working. Here No D398 is departing from Healey Mills Yard on 3 February 1968 whilst a Stanier Class 8F travels light engine in the background after arrival with a trip working from Rose Grove. *F. Bullock*

*Above:*
**Brush/Sulzer Type 4 No D1579 passes under Holgate Road bridge as it leaves York with a southbound express in July 1967. During their service on BR there have been numerous detail differences in this class as they were modified for a number of reasons.** *Derek Penney*

*Below:*
**This very rare colour picture taken at Darlington in the late 1950s apparently shows what became the standard BR Drewry 204hp diesel-mechanical 0-6-0 shunter undergoing dynamometer car trials.** *J. M. Jarvis*

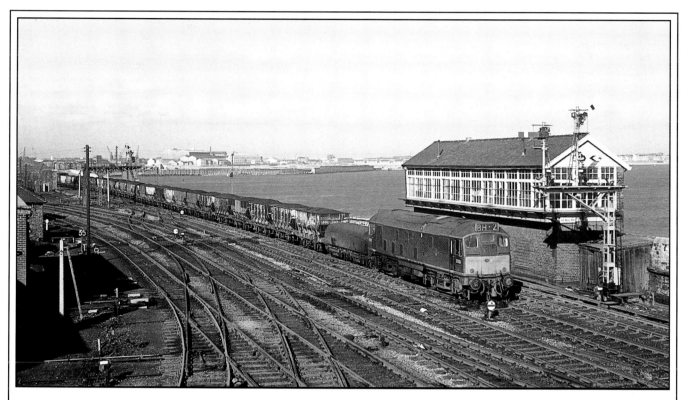

*Above:*
The weight of most early diesels gave rise to another problem, that of braking. Here, a BR/Sulzer Type 2 is paired with a brake tender as it hauls a coal train past Newburn, West Hartlepool, in 1964. *J. G. Dewing*

*Below:*
Another BR/Sulzer 1,160hp Type 2 No D5149, passes Manors, Newcastle upon Tyne, from the Heaton direction with a short freight on 21 May 1962. *M. Mensing*

*Below:*
**The viaduct carrying the Fort William line over the River Dochart is visible in this picture taken on 11 April 1970 as Class 27 No 5398 shunts wagons loaded with timber at Crianlarich.** *Dr L. A. Nixon*

*Bottom:*
**Still active on main line passenger duty. This picture taken north of Stonehaven in July 1966 depicts English Electric Type 4 No D265 working an Edinburgh to Aberdeen train.** *Derek Penney*

# FIVE

# Scottish Region

Born out of the railways of the former LMS and LNER, the Scottish Region was very determined to remove steam from the Highlands, the far north lines and parts of the Glasgow suburban area in the early 1960s. Dieselisation of the sinuous routes through the mountains was completed rapidly between 1960 and 1962.

One interesting feature of Scottish dieselisation not repeated elsewhere on BR was its decision to standardise on the Bo-Bo Type 2 as the predominant motive power for nearly all duties on main and branch lines that were not already in the hands of multiple-units. Though clearly more expensive, the Type 2s usually ran in pairs, giving the advantage of eight traction motors over the severe Scottish gradients instead of the six in a single Type 4. The Birmingham Railway Carriage & Wagon (BRCW) and BR Type 2s worked together indiscriminately on all types of duties. The 1,160hp locomotives tended to be used over the northern lines whilst the 1,250hp types were more often found on the West Highland and other routes.

One service that remained in the hands of steam motive power until the end of 1966 was the high speed 3hr inter-city service between Glasgow and Aberdeen, which was mainly entrusted to one of the ex-LNER Class A4 locomotives. At that time almost all inter-regional trains on both East and West coast routes were diesel hauled, whilst DMUs did sterling work on the east coast between Edinburgh and Dundee and in Lanarkshire and part of Ayrshire.

Inter-City cross-country-type DMUs achieved a high standard of performance between Inverness and Aberdeen, Edinburgh and Glasgow, and Glasgow and Ayr, while a number of freight train operating schemes worked by the Type 1 Clayton-Paxman 900hp locomotives and the Type 1 English Electric 1,000hp locomotives made considerable contributions to the operation of freight workings throughout the region.

Scotland was also the home of an active locomotive building industry which not only saw the production of the North British Locomotive Co (NBL) types of main line diesels in addition to the construction of numerous types of diesel shunting locomotives. The first of the North British 1,000hp diesels had left Queens Park works on 5 December 1958. Subsequent trials on the

Eastern Region with an eight-coach train took place on both 8 and 12 December, on the latter occasion the whole ensemble having to be dragged back to the works by a 'J11'. The first 10 locomotives of this type (D6100-9) were built as part of BR's pilot scheme and were initially allocated to Hornsey for use on Great Northern suburban duties.

Prior to the reallocation of the whole class to the Scottish Region, No D6130 made a trial trip over the West Highland on 12 November 1959, working the 6.45am Glasgow to Mallaig. Progress was lamentable, Mallaig being reached some 80 minutes late with subsequent delays to the MacBraynes steamers. On the return journey, No D6130 made even worse progress, arriving in Glasgow some two and a half hours late, the official excuse being 'It couldn't take to the hills', although a more likely reason was that the sanding gear had been defective on a day of heavy rain — a phenomenon not unknown on the West Highland.

After reallocation to Scotland various members of the class were prone to pyrotechnic displays. On 29 March 1962 No D6127 caught fire whilst working in multiple on the 3.15 Glasgow Buchanan Street to Dundee at Greenloaning, little above the bogies and frames being left intact.

In February 1962 a proposal was made to downgrade the D6100-37 series to Type 1s and rebuild them to resemble the D8000 series, thus improving all-round visibility and fitting them for freight work where their vagaries would be more acceptable. No D6130 probably entered Queens Park Works to estimate with such modification in mind, but was later sent out when closure of the works was announced on 3 April 1962.

With the gradual elimination of steam power and the contraction in the size of the rail network the main BR workshops in Scotland also suffered reductions in their workloads. Thus Inverurie, Barassie and Cowlairs works closed, the works at Townhill were converted to a wagon shop and only the St Rollox works of the former Caledonian Railway survived the effects of the 1962 workshop plan. Steam in Scotland was eliminated by the end of 1966, but the speed up of London to Glasgow expresses led to multiple diesel locomotive workings north of Crewe.

*Top:*
Seen crossing Liddel Water, south of Newcastleton on the Waverley route, English Electric Type 4 No D263 heads the 17.54 Edinburgh to Carlisle on 26 June 1968. At this time a work to rule meant that a number of trains from the West Coast line were diverted from the Glasgow/Edinburgh-Carlisle line via the Waverley route. *M. Mensing*

*Above:*
This very late view of English Electric Class 40 taken on 3 July 1978 sees No 40106 with its green livery barely visible leaving Ayr with 1M50 from Stranraer to Carlisle. No 40106 was the second Class 40 to enter preservation but the first to be returned to traffic and is currently based on the Nene Valley Railway at Peterborough. *Derek Cross*

*Above:*
**Clayton Equipment Co 900hp Bo-Bo Type 1s Nos D8526/D8519 stand at Beattock station prior to shunting an up goods working into the yard on 5 October 1963.** *Hugh Ballantyne*

*Below:*
**Ably assisted in the rear by one of Beattock's Fairburn 2-6-4Ts No 42125, English Electric Type 4 No D294 passes Greskine on the climb to Beattock summit with an oil train on 31 May 1966.** *Hugh Ballantyne*

*Right:*
Another English Electric Type 4 at work on the former Caledonian main line between Carlisle and Glasgow. Here, No D227 *Parthia* has charge of an up express composed of mainly former LMS stock at Abington on 28 August 1964. *N. Fields*

*Below:*
This picture taken at Motherwell MPD on 3 June 1963 sees a Clayton Type 1 receiving attention and a row of withdrawn Ministry of Supply 'Austerity' WD 2-10-0s dominate the background. Shed staff enjoy the sunshine outside the bothy and the body of an ex-Caledonian railway van is to be seen behind the buffer stops. *Ray Reed*

*Left:*
In this period picture taken at Glasgow Central on Bank Holiday Monday 23 May 1961, passengers waiting to board the 'Royal Scot' departure to London inspect the new form of motive power in the shape of an English Electric Type 4. The first of the production batch, No D211, had the distinction of being the first member of the class to arrive in Glasgow when it worked the 4.15pm Crewe to Glasgow Central on 19 August 1960. *Ray Reed*

*Above:*
**BRCW Co Type 2 No D5351 breasts the summit of the 1½-mile, 1 in 41 climb out of Glasgow Queen Street at Cowlairs, with what was probably a Fife coast train on 29 March 1964. There were some initial problems with the engines of these locomotives but after some modifications, the general design proved to be most satisfactory.** *Neville Simms*

*Below:*
**In this picture taken on the approach to Edinburgh Waverley a Gloucester Railway Carriage & Wagon Co two-car DMU (later Class 100) is seen passing through Princes Street Gardens on 8 June 1965.** *M. S. Welch*

*Above:*
**An unidentified BRCW Type 2 is seen passing the North British Railway signalbox at Dalmeny as it leaves the Forth Bridge with a short freight on 4 July 1964. It is interesting to note that together with the South Eastern Railway, the NBR was the only company to use sash cord windows in its signalboxes.** *R. Lissenden*

*Below:*
**In this 8 June 1962 picture, Type 2 diesels Nos D5124 and D5341 are approaching Dalmeny as they leave the Forth Bridge with an up express from Aberdeen. On the left of the picture the 40mph speed restriction indicator for the bridge can be seen.** *T. B. Owen*

*Left:*
An unidentified English Electric Type 4 passes Dundee Esplanade on the approach to the Tay Bridge with an Edinburgh train on 31 May 1966. The former Caledonian Railway depot survives as Dundee West diesel depot in the background. *Neville Fields*

*Left:*
Early dieselisation of services in the Edinburgh area utilised the Metro-Cammell three-car DMU sets which enabled interval services to be operated to Dundee, Kirkcaldy and Dunfermline, as well as along the main lines via Falkirk to Stirling and Glasgow. Here the front car is of Metro-Cammell origin as this two-car set passes Alloa West Junction on 28 May 1966. *Neville Fields*

*Below:*
Gleneagles railbus No SC79968 is seen at Crieff on 3 June 1960. This unit was one of five built by D. Wickham & Co Ltd, and was fitted with Andre Westinghouse pneumatic suspension in place of standard semi-elliptical axle-box springs. The Crieff to Gleneagles line closed to passengers from 6 July 1964 and to goods traffic from 2 November 1964. *F. Bullock*

Top:
This Oban to Glasgow (Queen Street) service is seen at Connel Ferry behind BRCW Type 2 No 5358 in June 1971. It can be seen that the second coach in the consist carries a miniature buffet. *Dr L. A. Nixon*

Above:
BRCW Type 2s Nos D5362 and D5357 are seen outside Oban shed in this general view taken on 5 August 1962. D5362 had worked the Ballachulish branch the day before. *Neville Simms*

*Top:*
**Through coaches from Mallaig are in the formation of the 5.45pm departure from Fort William in charge of English Electric Type 1s Nos D8104 and D8072, 2 July 1962. Today, Fort William station has been moved east in order to allow development of the old site.**
*Cliff Woodhead*

*Above:*
**English Electric Type 1 No D8110 and BRCW Type 2 No D5365 are seen outside the depot at Fort William on Saturday 4 August 1962. Today, No D8110 is preserved at the other end of the country on the South Devon Railway at Buckfastleigh.** *Neville Simms*

*Above:*
**BR/Sulzer Type 2 No D5127 is seen 1¼ miles west of Strome Ferry as it works the 5.40pm Inverness to Kyle of Lochalsh on 7 July 1965. Dieselisation of the sinuous routes through the mountains of the Scottish Region took place rapidly between 1960 and 1962 and was entrusted to the BRCW and BR/Sulzer Type 2s.** *M. Mensing*

*Below:*
**BRCW Type 2 No D5335 is shunting vans out of Kyle of Lochalsh station in this picture taken on 7 July 1965. This group of locomotives was later formed into Class 26 and Class 27 and whilst the Class 27 had a number of technical modifications they were easily distinguishable by their four-panel headcode box.** *M. Mensing*

*Left:*
A view of a down train on the line from Inverness to Wick as a BR/Sulzer Type 2 heads north past Golspie in September 1963. This train would be split at Georgemas Junction with the front portion going to Wick and the rear portion to Thurso. *M. S. Welch*

*Left:*
An interesting picture taken at Aberdeen station on 4 June 1965 as English Electric Type 4 No D262 prepares to depart with the 16.00 to Edinburgh. In the background, Stanier Class 5 No 44797 has its tender stacked high for another southbound departure. *Ken Fairey*

*Below:*
Near Cove Bay, south of Aberdeen, BR/Sulzer No D5114 has charge of the 17.25 Aberdeen to Glasgow (Buchanan Street) on Sunday 5 July 1964. *M. Mensing*

*Above:*
**In this picture BR 0-6-0 shunter No D3347 has charge of a short freight as it passes the signalbox at Montrose South on 30 May 1966. One week earlier on 22 May the line to Inverbervie had been closed in a blaze of glory, the local populace cramming the station platforms.** *Neville Fields*

*Below:*
**A dramatic late afternoon picture taken one mile northeast of Stonehaven as BRCW Type 2 No D5314 heads an empty stock train which includes some sleeping cars.** *M. Mensing*